CELEBRATING

It's A Wonderful Life

How the Movie's Message of Hope Lives On

Karolyn Grimes

"Zu Zu"

CELEBRATING

It's A Wonderful Life

How the Movie's Message of Hope Lives On

Karolyn "Zuzu" Grimes

Published by eChristian, Inc.
Escondido, California

Celebrating *It's a Wonderful Life*

eChristian, Inc.
2235 Enterprise Street, Suite 140
Escondido, CA 92029
http://echristian.com

ISBN: 978-1-61843-223-0

All movie quotes are from the screenplay of *It's a Wonderful Life*. © 1946 by Frances Goodrich, Albert Hackett, and Frank Capra Dorothy Parker, Dalton Trumbo, and Clifford Odets, with additional scenes by Jo Swerling. Based on "The Greatest Gift," an original short story by Philip Van Doren Stern.

Broadcast rights to *It's a Wonderful Life* are owned by Republic Entertainment, Inc., a subsidiary of Spelling Entertainment Group. Republic Entertainment has not approved or endorsed this publication.

The book on page 21 is *A Child's Book of Prayers*, published by Random House in 1941 © 1941 by Artists and Writers Guild, Inc.

The poem on page 45, "An All-Star Child Star," by Greg Asimakoupoulos. Used by permission.

The poem on page 97, "A Poem of Hope," by Christopher Ian Hill was originally printed in an e-mail to Karolyn Grimes. Used by permission.

Cover design by Larry Taylor
Interior design by Mark Wainwright and Larry Taylor
Project Coordinator: Afton Rorvik
Project Staff: Molly Anderson, Katie Arnold, Dan Balow, Joel Bartlett, Andy Culbertson, Claudia Gerwin, Lois Jackson, Tom Shumaker, Linda Taylor, and Linda Washington

Images from the movie *It's a Wonderful Life* are courtesy of the Collection of Richard Goodson. Other photos come from the collection of Karolyn Grimes. All trademarks and identifying images are owned and controlled by their various owners. All mentions and images are used in this format as a journalistic and entertainment endeavor. No infringement, right, title, license or interest is implied. Images are representations of said collection and are lent as such. Use of any image is not to be considered affiliation with, or endorsement by, any controlling interest.

Printed in the United States of America

19 18 17 16 15 14 13 12   8 7 6 5 4 3 2 1

Dedication

I would like to dedicate this book

to all the wonderful people who worked on this film

and those who have found meaning in the

film's many messages of hope.

KG

5

FOREWORD

I first met Karolyn Grimes on the set of *It's a Wonderful Life*. She was Zuzu, and I was her little brother Tommy Bailey, the one who kept saying, "'Scuse me, 'scuse me . . . I burped."

In between shots we'd run around the set to explore all its wonders. All that real snow on the stage around the Bailey house—not something we usually saw in California. It was June 1946, and 90 degrees outside. We shot all the Bailey family scenes in 12 days at the RKO Pathe Studios in Culver City on stage 14. After the wrap party (which was a picnic out at Lake Malibu), I never saw Karolyn for 46 years. She left Hollywood and moved away to Kansas.

February, 1993… We were asked by the Target Stores to help promote their *IAWL* Christmas theme. They wanted to make an impact and do something really special to get the attention of their customers. So they rounded up The Bailey kids and sent us on a promotional tour. All of a sudden the *Wonderful Life* siblings were re-united. There was Janie (Carol Coombs Mueller), Peter (Larry Simms) and "little Zuzu"(Karolyn)…WOW….. We had a lot of years to catch up on. Wherever we went there were crowds lined around the stores. They loved meeting us . . . especially Zuzu. Since then, Karolyn and I have become very close. We call each other and email often. Thank God for Target.

These days Karolyn continues to share *It's a Wonderful Life's*

Jimmy and Karolyn at a signing for Walgreens at the Empire State building

enduring message of hope, charity, and life renewed to the thousands of people she meets each year all over the country. Through her passion for the classic movie, they are made aware of what George Bailey learned: what really counts in life are the things you can't put a price tag on— family, friends, and the belief in miracles.

What impresses me about Karolyn? Her wonderful life enthusiasm. She always has a smile and time to listen to the movie's fans. When she's with them, it is as if they are the only one in the room. She embodies the *It's a Wonderful Life's* theme, "Each man's life touches so many others. If they weren't around, it would leave an awful hole."

This book is a tribute to Karolyn for winning the part of Zuzu and using her fame to bring such encouragement to so many. She has truly touched lives and for the better.

Attagirl, Karolyn!

With great affection,
Jimmy Hawkins
Los Angeles, CA

Jimmy Hawkins is an American actor and film producer whose career began as a child actor with such Hollywood stars as Spencer Tracy, Lana Turner, James Stewart, and Donna Reed. His acting career spans from 1944–1968, after which he devoted his energies to production of films. In 1961, Jimmy was voted into the Academy of Motion Pictures Arts and Sciences. He has written five popular books on the classic film, It's a Wonderful Life.

Introduction

In 1946, when *It's a Wonderful Life* debuted, the cast and director, Frank Capra, had little idea that it would one day become one of the most beloved films of all time. It opened to lukewarm reviews and was deemed a failure at the box office. Though it earned several Oscars nominations, it wound up zero for five. Decades later, in a three-hour special television event, which aired June 14, 2006, the American Film Institute jury of 1,500 film artists, critics, and historians selected the classic *It's a Wonderful Life*, starring James Stewart, as the most inspiring movie of all time. This film, about a man at the end of his rope who learns the value of his life through a guardian angel, has touched the lives of countless viewers.

Final poster for advertising the film

Jimmy Stewart and Donna Reed posing for the poster illustration

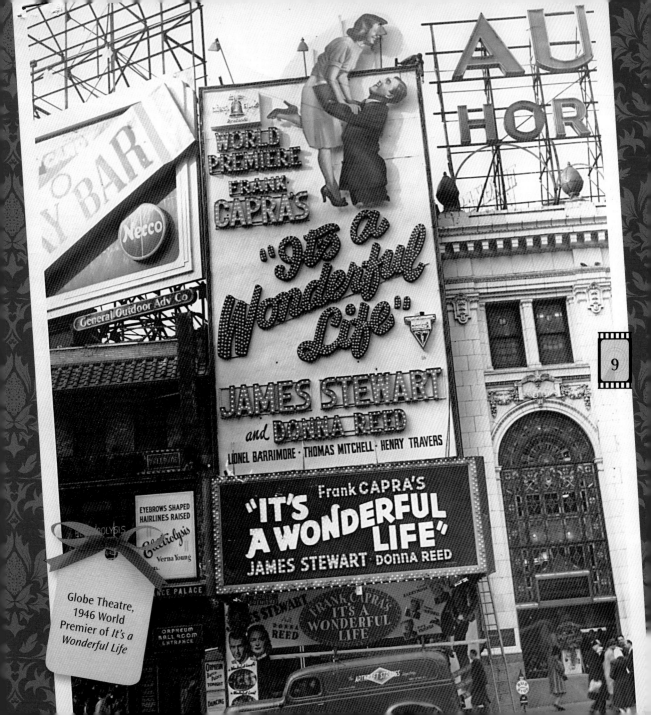

Globe Theatre, 1946 World Premier of *It's a Wonderful Life*

9

L to R: Carol Coombs Mueller, Bobby Anderson, who played young George Bailey, Jimmy Hawkins, and Karolyn Grimes

*F*or me, being Zuzu is a gift. It has given me the opportunity to meet so many people and hear their stories of surviving the hurdles of life. I am so lucky to have this chance to touch peoples' lives and share the gift I was given by being in this movie.

Through the pages of this book, I want to share that gift with you. I hope that these stories will touch you as they have touched me. And I hope that the photos, recipes, and bits of trivia will put a smile on your face and pull you back to the sights and sounds of Bedford Falls and the joy of family and friends.

Karolyn Grimes
"Zuzu"

Candid shot of the Bailey family

Karolyn, age 3

AUGUST 2, 2012

I connected with Karolyn completely by accident and completely embarrassingly funny, at least for me. I was sitting in my public relations office reading The Detroit News *in the fall of 1995. There was a three-sentence blurb in it about Karolyn living a wonderful life in Overland Park, Kansas. I told my wife, Jean, I was going to call information and see if her number was listed. The conversation with her went something like this, but keep in mind the IAWL is my favorite movie of all times:*

"Jeanie, there's a piece in today's paper about Karolyn Grimes from IAWL and it lists the city where she lives."

"So, you're just going to call info and get her number? Then what, Chief?"

"Then I'll call her to say hi and introduce myself."

"What makes you think she is listed much less want to talk to you?"

"I'm a PR man. I'll figure it out as I go."

Sure enough, there was a Karolyn Grimes Wilkerson listed and I got the number. I sat there after hanging up with information, not knowing what to do. Here I had in my possession a phone number for someone I had adored for years, and in multiple films.

"Now what, Slick?" Jean asked.

13

Well, that was a challenge in my book, so I called. All I got was a recording so I nervously hung up. I waited about 30 minutes and decided to try again. My wife was laughing at this point! I dialed the number and here is how it kind of went:

"Hello," came this nice voice on the other end of the line.

"Um, er, ah, is this um Karolyn Grimes?"

"Yes."

"Karolyn Grimes."

"Yes!" (I could already tell she was annoyed but having sport with me!)

14

"Weren't you, um, ah . . ."

"Yes!" she said cutting me off.

"And didn't you . . . ah, um . . ."

"Yes!" she said again cutting me off again in an attempt to help me get the words out without stammering too much.

"So you were Zuzu?"

"Yes. What do you want?" she asked.

"Well, I . . . um . . ." Silence. "I don't know," I blurted out.

"Well you must want something. You called me, remember?"

Continued on page 16

LIBERTY FILMS INC.

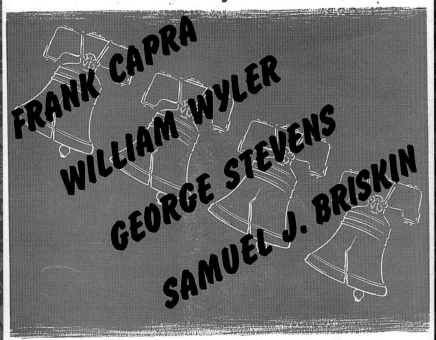

FRANK CAPRA

WILLIAM WYLER

GEORGE STEVENS

SAMUEL J. BRISKIN

Now in Production: Frank Capra's "It's A Wonderful Life," starring James Stewart & Donna Reed, with Lionel Barrymore, Thomas Mitchell, Beulah Bondi, Ward Bond, Frank Faylen, Henry Travers, Gloria Grahame, H. B. Warner.

Now in Preparation: George Stevens' "One Big Happy Family." A Gay Romantic Comedy by Joseph Fields will go into Production Late in 1946.

Now in Prospect: William Wyler has reported to Liberty Films and he will shortly announce his first production for release in 1947.

Poster advertising
Liberty Films

LIBERTY FILMS Inc.
RELEASED THROUGH RKO-RADIO PICTURES

Well, I finally took a deep breath and calmed down, and explained that I was a PR specialist and thought that maybe we could work together or something. She asked, "On what?"

I had no idea, but told her I would call her right back. I happened to have some clients that owned a nostalgia store in Royal Oak, Michigan called Decades. They specialized in all sorts of cool things. I immediately called them up and told them to whom I had just spoken and that I was going to turn their tiny store into Bedford Falls, a la Michigan. They both said I was nuts, but I persisted. They finally relented.

I called Karolyn back and told her I had lined up a special appearance for her in my hometown and she agreed to fly up. The day of the event we had people waiting for three short city blocks to see her. We had the mayor give her the key to the city at City Hall, we had a choir singing Christmas carols, and the store ran out of anything resembling angels, rose petals, etc. And the entire time I had the worst bronchitis I had had in years. But I wasn't going to let that ruin the moment!

The event was so successful that while driving Karolyn back to the airport I believe I was the one who approached her about representing her for PR endeavors. She came back two or three other times after that.

But the story gets better, as one of the guys from the Nostalgia store knew a book buyer at Carol Publishing. We came up with an idea for a

IAWL Cookbook filled with recipes, photos, and trivia and they bought it! We had a blast doing the book, and still get royalties, albeit small, to this day. I got to speak with several people from the movie who were still alive at the time. Way cool!

My next book with my publisher was a cat book called The Cats of Our Lives, and Karolyn has an excellent cat rescue story in it.

Karolyn and I have remained very close throughout the years and I feel like I touched a piece of history. (Note: Karolyn's version of this story may be a little different and even more funny!)

Cordially,
Franklin Dohanyos
Franklin Publicity, Inc.

Franklin Dohanyos
and his wife Jean

PHOTO FROM FRANKLIN DOHANYOS

LIBERTY FILMS

Presents

FRANK CAPRA'S

"IT'S A WONDERFUL LIFE"

starring

JAMES STEWART

and

DONNA REED

with

LIONEL BARRYMORE

THOMAS MITCHELL

HENRY TRAVERS

BEULAH BONDI

WARD BOND

FRANK FAYLEN

GLORIA GRAHAME

H. B. WARNER
SAMUEL S. HINDS
FRANK ALBERTSON
VIRGINIA PATTON
TODD KARNS

Released by RKO Radio Pictures, Inc.

Produced and Directed by - - - FRANK CAPRA

Screen Play by - - - - - - - FRANCES GOODRICH
ALBERT HACKETT
FRANK CAPRA

Additional Scenes by - - - - - JO SWERLING

18

"IT'S A WONDERFUL LIFE"

* * *

CAST AND CREDITS

George Bailey	JAMES STEWART
Mary Hatch	DONNA REED
Potter	LIONEL BARRYMORE
Uncle Billy	THOMAS MITCHELL
Mrs. Bailey	BEULAH BONDI
Ernie	FRANK FAYLEN
Bert	WARD BOND
Clarence	HENRY TRAVERS
Mr. Gower	H. B. WARNER
Violet	GLORIA GRAHAME
Harry Bailey	TODD KARNS
Ruth Dakin	VIRGINIA PATTON
Pa Bailey	SAMUEL S. HINDS
Cousin Millie	MARY TREEN
Cousin Eustace	CHARLES WILLIAMS
Mrs. Hatch	SARA EDWARDS
Mr. Martini	BILL EDMUNDS
Annie	LILLIAN RANDOLPH
Sam Wainwright	FRANK ALBERTSON
Mrs. Martini	ARGENTINA BRUNETTI
Little George	BOBBIE ANDERSON
Little Sam	RONNIE RALPH
Little Mary	JEAN GALE
Little Violet	JEANNIE ANN ROOSE
Little Marty Hatch	DANNY MUNERT
Little Harry Bailey	GEORGIE NOAKS
Nick	SHELDON LEONARD
Potter's Bodyguard	FRANK HAGNEY

Joe (luggage shop)..............................RAY WALKER

Real Estate Salesman........................,.CHARLIE LANE

Tom (Bldg. & Loan)............................EDWARD KEAN

The Bailey Children:

    Janie....................................CAROL COOMES

    Zuzu.....................................KAROLYN GRIMES

    Pete.....................................LARRY SIMMS

    Tommy...................................JIMMY HAWKINS

*   *   *

Director of Photography-----------Joseph Walker, A.S.C.
                           Joseph Biroc

Art Director------------------------------------Jack Okey

Set Decorations--------------------------------Emile Kuri

Music Written & Directed by-------------Dimitri Tiomkin

Edited by---------------------------------William Hornbeck

Sound by---------------------------------Richard Van Hessen

Gowns by---------------------------------Edward Stevenson

Assistant Director----------------------Arthur S. Black

Fade In

GOWER'S VOICE:

I owe everything to George Bailey. Help him, dear Father.

MARTINI'S VOICE:

Joseph, Jesus, and Mary. Help my friend Mr. Bailey.

MRS. BAILEY'S VOICE:

Help my son George tonight.

BERT'S VOICE:

He never thinks about himself, God; that's why he's in trouble.

ERNIE'S VOICE:

George is a good guy. Give him a break, God.

MARY'S VOICE:

I love him, dear Lord. Watch over him tonight.

Zuzu

The first book I ever got as a child was for
Christmas. It was an angel book of prayers.

A Child's Book
of Prayers

I have never forgotten
that lovely book, and I
still have it today.

This is one of my favorite childhood prayers:

Here I Lay Me

Here I lay me down to sleep.
I pray the Lord my soul to keep;
And if I die before I wake,
I pray the Lord my soul to take.

There are four corners on my bed,
There are four angels at my head.
Matthew, Mark, Luke and John,
Bless the bed that I lie on.

Prayer from
A Child's Book of Prayers

Karolyn Grimes

JANIE'S VOICE:

Please, God. Something's the matter with Daddy.

I believe deeply in the power of prayer, and have ever since I asked the Lord Jesus to be my Savior and I became His child. I ask for His will to be done, and not just my desires.

Carol Coombs Mueller (Janie)

PRAYER

n. An address (as a petition) to God or a god in word or thought.

Merriam Webster's Collegiate Dictionary

*W*e became aware that Karolyn Grimes lived in our area, when the Kansas City Star did a feature story on her on Christmas Day, 1993.

About a year later in early 1995, my wife Ruth and I met Karolyn after I sent her a copy of my closing argument in a civil wrongful death case, where I compared the widow's deceased husband to George Bailey as he died helping someone else. Many neighbors and friends testified about what an unselfish friend he was, helping others to the point where he hadn't built up enough wealth for himself to survive a farming crisis in Missouri; and he and his wife were probably going to go bankrupt, even if he did live. Although the defense attorney challenged my George Bailey analogy, the jury "got it," and they brought back a substantial courtroom verdict. . . .

25

My wife and I extended an invitation to treat Karolyn to a nice dinner that we hoped, but really didn't think, she'd accept. But Karolyn did accept. When we met Karolyn at Martini's in Overland Park, KS, we were immediately struck by her star quality and charisma. She was so genuine that when she invited us and our children back to her house to see her collection of movie artifacts, we jumped at the chance.

After looking longingly at her amazing collection of artifacts from her movie career, she proceeded to give our two daughters specially made Zuzu dolls. These 18-inch replicas of little Zuzu in her red plaid nightgown with a rosebud accessory thrilled us as much as our daughters. We literally gulped when she gave us two of them, as she mentioned that just one had sold at recent cancer fundraiser for $1,800.

Zuzu dolls on display

We drove home and immediately climbed up in our attic at 10:00 at night to put up a display of our own meager IAWL artifact collection. This collection had been started several years earlier when Target began their promotion of the movie items. The little stuffed lamb with the bell attached to his neck, a popcorn tin with the IAWL movie scene on it and a golden medallion ornament of Zuzu, George and Uncle Billy around the tree were among the treasures found by my wife and my mom. That was the beginning of our huge It's a Wonderful Life collection and an ongoing friendship with Karolyn over the years. It resulted in trips as Karolyn's "entourage" to Jimmy Stewart's and Donna Reed's museums for the movie's 50-year anniversary and annual trips to Seneca Falls, New York for the IAWL weekend there. . . .

As president of the Zuzu Society, I have talked to seemingly calm autograph collectors standing in line to see Zuzu, only to see them break down sobbing as they shared their own personal story of despair and the redemptive effect of the movie on them, with her, "Zuzu!" Her caring responses and kind smile seem to have a very therapeutic effect.

As one of the few living stars left from the vintage movie classic, Karolyn has taken on the mantle of movie ambassador, as people literally stand in line for hours in the cold, waiting for an autographed picture, a brief moment sharing their experience of the movie, and a photograph, graciously provided by Karolyn. From the first autograph to the last, both her handwriting and her demeanor bear no evidence of fatigue or boredom. Each fan receives Karolyn's full and undivided attention.

The essence of her movie charm and her sincere, caring manner has won her fans around the globe. . . . I truly feel that we have a wonderful life, having been blessed knowing Karolyn since 1995.

> *John Mencl*
> *President of Zuzu Society*

Karolyn and Chris
with Ruth and John Mencl

Karolyn autographing photos for her fans

June 7, 2012

One of the quotes in the movie that means the most to me is, "Please bring daddy back. . . ."

I connected with Karolyn through her Zuzu newsletter. I read some of the stories as to how the movie influenced different individuals' lives. I was going through a rough time then and my letter was printed. Now, almost 18 years later, I have come through it all. <u>It's a Wonderful Life</u> has a recurring theme of hope and redemption as symbolized by family and bells. I always thought of the "bell" theme as an acronym for "Blessed Echoes Lucidly Lingering."

As a father, I know that our children do "bring us back" from the perils of that precipitous journey through life. When we reach the abyss, their voices echo, "Please bring Daddy back. . . ."

My wife Beth and I have five children and seven grandchildren. They are all our "blessed" gifts whose voices "echo" the joys of life to such fervor that their "lucid" tones "linger" with us forever.

Terry Deinlein

ZUZU'S VOICE:

Please bring Daddy back.

SCENE
One

JOSEPH'S VOICE:
George saved his brother's life that day. But he caught a bad cold which infected his left ear. Cost him his hearing in that ear. It was weeks before he could return to his after-school job at old man Gower's drugstore.

Zuzu

I remember the day...

I remember the day my mother took me to interview for the part of Zuzu. She dressed me to look "picture-book perfect" with my hair up in a bunch of little bun curls. Then we took the streetcar to the studio. There were five or six other girls in the room and this was serious stuff. One of the moms "accidentally" spilled coffee on my dress. Funny, I don't remember getting upset. I think it might actually have helped me land the part because it gave me something to talk about!

I was six at the time most of my scenes were filmed. Honestly, I didn't think much about it. It was like going to school. I just did what they told me to do. It was a job. I made $75 dollars a day! (My mother saved my pay stub.) I do remember that when Frank Capra wanted to give me directions, he always got down on his knees and talked to me at eye level.

Karolyn at age 4

What a childhood! I had roles in 16 movies and got to know some amazing people as friends—Fred MacMurray, Bing Crosby, Jimmy Stewart, Angela Lansbury, Cary Grant, Cecil B. DeMille, John Wayne, and Danny Kaye.

And then when I was about ten, life started to change. I was growing up; so I was getting too old for some parts. And then television came along. Some people thought that meant the end of movies.

My mother also started to decline mentally. I think now that she had early onset Alzheimer's. Her last years were so hard for all of us.

My father and I had a special relationship that was formed when my mother started getting ill. For eight years, we had both watched as she slowly faded away in front of our very eyes. In truth, I lost my mother when I was eight years old. My father did everything possible to make her life comfortable. She lived with us in our home until her death. He hired folks to come

Karolyn's acting dues and work permit. Notice the signature on the check by her mom.

in during the day and she was able to close her eyes for the last time in her own bed. For that, I will always be grateful to my father because of his dedicated love for her.

However, living with her and her illness was hard on an only child whose mother doted on her and even pursued a career for her in the motion picture industry. I soon learned we are not always handed a "pass go" card to enjoy your good fortune.

What a childhood!

However, on the positive side it was an experience that helped me prepare for the life that was to come my way. Sometimes I had to stick up for myself just the way that George did for his father against Mr. Potter.

Karolyn, her parents, and her dog Cisco

38

My mother died when I was 14. My acting career seemed to die then too. I did a few things for television that I don't even remember well. Mostly, I just lived the life of a teenager in California.

I had been cradled from the real world and when I began to see that I was going to be alone and not have the comfort of my mother, I had to grow up and face all the emotional turmoil that a teenager had to experience. Dealing with all the hormones thrashing about inside me, was hard on my father, and for that I am really sorry.

Mr. Peter Bailey had to tussle with old man Potter much of his life, and he always fought back. His way was to be gentle and to help his fellow man to have better lives, not obligated to a person who was just interested in taking their last dime. I have tried to practice dealing with difficult people with patience and firmness throughout my life.

I do remember going on a tryout interview when I was 15 to play the role of Ricky Nelson's girlfriend on The Adventures of *Ozzie and Harriet*. I found out much later that Jimmy Hawkins, who played Tommy in *It's a Wonderful Life*, won the part of Ricky's friend.

Instead of getting the phone call announcing that I had won the part, I got a phone call from a family friend who had been on a trip with my father. Now my father was always playing practical jokes. So at first I thought this phone call was a joke. Then I heard words I never expected to hear: "I have some really sad news for you. Your father is dead."

Karolyn's mother, Martha Grimes

Gradually the truth sank in over the next few days. I was an orphan. Then within six days after my father's car accident, I was in a car with my aunt and uncle, traveling to their home in Osceola, Missouri.

My Hollywood days began to fade quickly as I learned to adjust to life with my guardians in a small, Midwest town. For me, it was a culture change and I had to be mature and endure. I ended up living with my father's brother and his difficult wife. For years, my endurance and tolerance was tested. My lifeline was my thread of prayers to God that permeated my life. Those were my mantra and my "Clarence" was watching over me, of that I am sure.

Karolyn Grimes
"Zu Zu"

I was a bashful, shy country boy who was blind in one eye and had cataracts in the other eye. A lot of the kids bullied me, but not Karolyn. She was nice to me. She helped me with reading. I think I helped her with algebra because I could do that in my head.

She came back for a high school reunion one year, and I bought one of her books then. That's when I discovered that she had been in the movie *It's a Wonderful Life*. I didn't even know about the movie until then. Now I watch it every year. I always tease Karolyn that I am in that movie with her—as Clarence. I love that part of the movie when Clarence the angel appears and tries to teach George something.

Karolyn and I talk on the phone every couple of months. I like to tell her jokes and make her laugh. We both have July birthdays. I know she didn't have such a wonderful life, but she is such a nice person.

Email from Clarence Gillespie

Karolyn with her high school friend Clarence

Once my son got in trouble in middle school, and the school prinicpal said that she was really sad that he had made a bad choice, because basically she believed he was a good kid and didn't deserve the big gun. So, she called me in and told me, in his presence, that his punishment was to watch It's a Wonderful Life. She said that she wanted him to think carefully about every decision that he made in life because one person could make such a difference in the world. I thought that she was pretty wise, and I so appreciated her understanding because he was a good kid.

—Donna Marie Loverette

42

Dear Karolyn

For years I have been watching *It's a Wonderful Life* and every year at the same time on December 24 me and my grandma watch it. I am now 13, and don't spend as much time as I used to with her, but we still follow through with the tradition. . . . Today we gathered around and passing through my mind was how wonderful everyone looked and how my great-grandma was in heaven with her wings, and I opened a package from my grandma. It was the colored film of *It's a Wonderful Life* and of course the black and white one as well :) It even had a bell on it. It made me so happy.

It truly is a wonderful life,

> Yours truly,
> Brittney Magnuson

An All-Star Child Star

It's a wonderful life
quite apart from the strife
that we cannot avoid in this world.
Such a claim is the truth
and you are living proof
looking back to when you were a girl.

Zuzu Bailey was blessed
but just who could have guessed
what awaited the young rising star?
Wilted flowers and pain
soon replaced treasured fame,
And although you would heal
you'd be scarred.

But your scars gave you wings.
You found lyrics to sing
And your petals (once dead) lived again.
You were loved through the night.
Seems that Clarence was right.
No one fails in this life who has friends.

Greg Asimakoupoulos

45

ZUZU'S *Sneak Peek*

*I*f you look closely at the scene when Mary leans over the counter to whisper in George's bad ear, you can see a piece of tape on the counter. Capra put that there to tell Mary where to lean. He forgot to take it out in the final edit. There is a lot of poor editing in this film, because it was a rush job. RKO had told Capra that his movie was supposed to be released in March or April of 1947. But they came to him right before Christmas and said, "You've got to get your movie ready and it is going to be the film for Christmas from the studio, because *Sinbad the Sailor* isn't ready yet. So hop to it, get it finished and get it out there." I'm not sure how long he had, but it wasn't very long. He put it together the best he could and it was released on December 20, which was really too late, at the Globe Theatre in New York.

PHOTOS FROM THE COLLECTION OF RICHARD GOODSON

George's Ice Cream Delight

2 cups crushed Rice or Corn Chex
1 cup shredded coconut
½ cup chopped pecans
⅔ cups brown sugar
½ cup melted butter

....

Mix ingredients. Place about two thirds of this mixture in a
9″ × 13″ pan. Pat down well. Spread over this crust a softened
½ gallon of any flavor ice cream. Sprinkle remaining crumb
mixture over top and place in freezer.

GEORGE (SOBBING):

Mr. Gower, you don't know what you're doing. You put something wrong in those capsules. I know you're unhappy. You got that telegram, and you're upset. You put something bad in those capsules. It wasn't your fault, Mr. Gower. . . .

48

Mr. Gower, I won't ever tell anyone. I know what you're feeling.
I won't ever tell a soul. Hope to die, I won't. . . .

CLARENCE'S VOICE:

. . . Tell me, did he ever tell anyone about the pills?

JOSEPH'S VOICE:

Not a soul.

*M*y children have never known a Thanksgiving evening without a viewing of *It's a Wonderful Life*. We've made this a family tradition, in the company of several other neighborhood families, for more than 13 years now.

This past Thanksgiving saw 15 children and 10 adults parked on our den floor watching *IAWL*. Of course, I shed a few tears—on cue, like I do every year. What a wonderful way to get our minds "tuned" for the Christmas season.

Thank you, Ms. Grimes, for this wonderful "wonderful" gift. Our door is always open to you if you want to watch IAWL with a bunch of delightful children some Thanksgiving evening in North Carolina. ;)

Tim Pennigar

$\mathcal{M}$y name is Jeff McCann, I'm a 35-year-old father of 7. Our life hasn't always been wonderful, but we do okay! :) I am currently enrolled in University taking a Bachelor of Science while my wife works full-time. Our children are all fans of your amazing movie, and i just wanted to drop you a line and thank you personally for the part you played in bringing *It's a Wonderful Life* to everyone. I'm a big softie at Christmas and this is always a tradition in our house, along with many others. Someday I hope to start collecting memorbilia from this movie to pass down to our children, if there's any left? :)

Blessings to you, and thanks again for your legacy.

Jeff McCann

SCENE ~~CENE~~ *Two*

GEORGE: Big—see! I don't want one for one night. I want something for a thousand and one nights, with plenty of room for labels from Italy and Baghdad, Samarkand . . . a great big one.

JOE: I see, a flying carpet, huh? I don't suppose you'd like this old second-hand job, would you?

GEORGE: Now you're talkin'. Gee whiz, I could use this as a raft in case the boat sunk. How much does this cost?

JOE: No charge.

GEORGE: That's my trick ear, Joe. It sounded as if you said, "no charge."

JOE (indicating name on suitcase): That's right.

GEORGE (as he sees his name): What's my name doing on it?

JOE: A little present from old man Gower. Came over and picked it out himself.

PHOTO FROM THE COLLECTION OF RICHARD GOODSON

Zuzu

I lost my family

Within days of my father's death, I was in a town (Osceola, Missouri) with a population of 800—fewer people in it than in my class at Los Angeles High School. I lost my family, my house, my school, my friends, my home—virtually my life. . . .

I remember asking people, "Do I have any voice in this? Can I say who I want to live with?" I didn't. My father's lawyer told me that I could keep only what was absolutely mine. That wasn't much. The relatives packed up the rest of it, including some of the memorabilia from my movies. At least I had my dog, Cisco.

My aunt seemed to have a rule for everything. I tried talking back and all the things teenagers do, but then I just gave up and became sort of a mouse. To be honest, I'm not really sure my aunt and uncle wanted to have me. And I really wanted to go back to Hollywood. In fact, I used to fantasize that someone like my boyfriend or friends of my parents would come and take me home.

Letters home to
Daddy while
making the film
"Rio Grande"

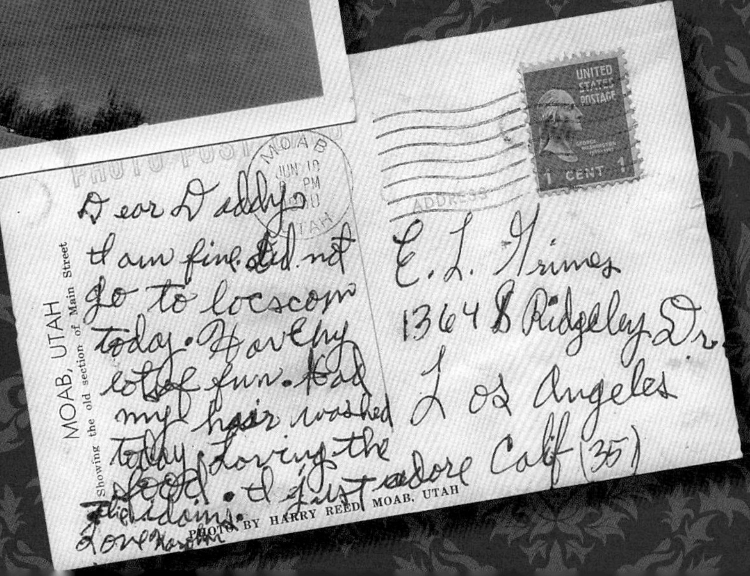

Marilyn Grimes
Moab Utah

MOAB
JUN 17
1950
UTAH

Mrs. E. L. Grimes
364 Ridgeley Dr.
S.
Los Angeles Calif 36

55

MOAB, UTAH
Showing the old section of Main Street.

PHOTO POST

MOAB
JUN 19
1950
UTAH

UNITED
STATES
POSTAGE
1 CENT 1

ADDRESS

Dear Daddy
I am fine. Did not
go to locscom
today. Have by
lot of fun. Had
my hair washed
today. Loving the
need. I just adore
Indians.
Love Marilyn

E. L. Grimes
364 S Ridgeley Dr.
Los Angeles
Calf (35)

PHOTO BY HARRY REED MOAB, UTAH

As I grew older, I learned to live the life of a teenager in a small town. Even though my guardians were so hard to live with, my teachers and people in the town went out of their way to encourage me. No one seemed to remember my movie days. They just thought of me as Karolyn. That was actually kind of nice.

I went to college for a year, married, had children, and worked as a medical technician. My life in Hollywood seemed so far away.

Karolyn and her father shortly before his death

Karolyn's high school
graduation photo

GEORGE:

Well, not just one wish. A whole hatful, Mary.
I know what I'm going to do tomorrow and the next
day and the next year and the year after that. I'm
shaking the dust of this crummy little town off my
feet and I'm going to see the world. Italy, Greece, the
Parthenon, the Colosseum. Then I'm coming back
here and go to college and see what they know . . . and
then I'm going to build things. I'm gonna build air
fields. I'm gonna build skyscrapers a hundred stories
high. I'm gonna build bridges a mile long.

*I*f you look carefully at the scene later in the movie when George gets so angry that he yells at his wife and kids and throws things around the house, you can see a model of a city with a skyscraper and large bridge sitting on a table. Clearly George still had his dream to build things, even if it was only models. When George destroyed that, Capra, in his genius way, is saying that this was the point when George Bailey lost hope.

59

JOSEPH'S VOICE:

. . . Not only that, but he gave his school money to his brother Harry, and sent him to college. Harry became a football star—made second team All American . . . George got four years older, waiting for Harry to come back and take over the Building and Loan.

Bailey's Brisket

1 well-trimmed out beef brisket
Sea salt
Pepper

....

Generously rub brisket with salt and pepper. Place brisket in oven
pan fat side up. I use a broiler pan. Bake uncovered 30 minutes at 450
degrees. Lower oven temperature to 225 degrees and bake brisket 1 hour
per pound. Remove, cool and put in refrigerator until cold.

Sauce
1 cup catsup
⅓ cup Worcestershire Sauce
¾ cup sugar
1 Tbsp lemon juice

....

Add enough water to meat juices in pan to make 2 cups. Stir well and
add 1 cup catsup, Worcestershire Sauce, sugar, and lemon juice. Stir well.
Place in jar and refrigerate. When chilled, skim off fat from top. When
serving, remove brisket and slice very thin while cold. Place in a large
shallow pan and cover with sauce. Cover pan with foil and heat in oven
at 300 degrees about 1 hour or until hot.

Enjoy!

*F*rank Capra was well-known for his family movies and his sentimental movies. The critics finally starting calling his movies "corny"and eventually "Capra-corn." In this movie, Harry Bailey's wife (Virginia Patton) gets off the train and walks right over and buys some popcorn and starts eating it with white gloves on. I think Capra was saying, "I know this is more of my Capra-corn."

Karolyn with
Frank Capra III

Behind the scenes with Frank
Capra and Jimmy Stewart

63

Marshmallow Capra-corn Squares

1 stick butter
1 package miniature marshmallows (10 oz)
8 cups popped corn
1 cup mixed nuts (optional)
2 cups M&Ms

....

Grease a 2-quart pan with olive oil. Use a large nonstick saucepan and melt butter over medium heat. Add marshmallows. Continue to heat and stir with a wooden spoon until mixture is melted.

Remove from heat. Add popped corn and nuts; stir to combine. Mix in candies. Press into greased pan. Cover with plastic wrap. Chill at least 2 hours and remove from pan. Cut into 1-inch pieces using a sharp knife.

ZUZU'S *Sneak Peek*

All you can take with you is that which you've given away.

This is a memorable moment in the film. When there is a run on the bank, George pauses a moment and glances at his father's portrait and the sign under it. Carrying forward his father's values, he gives his honeymoon money to the people.

When a loved one passes on, I often think of George Bailey and how our lives would be different without someone having ever been born. I feel the same way every time a new baby comes into our family and I think about how many lives that person will shape and form over the years ahead.

Deryk Houston

Karolyn at Walgreen's House

SEPTEMBER 12, 2002

I reside in New York, and yesterday was especially difficult as it was for the whole country. Just hearing from you made my day. Just to know that you exist reinforces my belief in the human spirit!

I had my little niece watch *It's a Wonderful Life* and she loved it too, and it has become a family favorite with her now as well.

Regards from a true, loyal fan,
Denise

A tribute to Jimmy

Zuzu

JAMES STEWART

Dear Jerry Baker —
Thanks you again for
your very kind and
thoughtful letter.
It's a Wonderful Life is my favorite.

Sincerely *James Stewart*

My friend Ted said, "I've got this friend [Jerry] and he lives in Illinois . . . in an apartment, but he had a whole room that is a tribute to Jimmy Stewart. He's been my friend for a long time. If there's anything I could give him it would be a surprise trip from you for Christmas. Would there be any way for me to do that?"

I said I would go.

Then I found out that Jerry and his wife hosted a *Wonderful Life* Party every year. So when I was next in Chicago for a "gig," and he was having his party, I knocked on the door, and said, "Does Jerry Baker live here?"

And he said, "I'm Jerry Baker."

And I said, "Does this rose in my hand mean anything to you?" I thought he was going to come unglued. . . . So I walk in—I didn't know any people in there in the party; it was just a small party. He took me in to see his Jimmy Stewart shrine. Oh, WOW! It was something else.

And over the years—his birthday is July 5, mine is July 4—Jerry and I became friends. And every time I go to Chicago I thought I'd look up Jerry. . . . I invited him to my house to see my stuff. So he and his wife came. He walked into the room where I had all my memorabilia and he looked at the empty yellow box of ginger snaps that I have and said, "Oh, my Gosh! Here's the ginger snaps! Here's the ginger snaps! That's where the name Zuzu came from!"

Ads for Zu Zu Ginger Snaps — "Zuzu, my little gingersnap."

Karolyn with her friend Jerry Baker

It's a Wonderful Life holds a special meaning to me. As a young man, I spent several years hunting down the kids from the film in the hopes of collecting their autographs. After several years of poor results, I turned to Mr. Stewart and asked if he could help me. (We were pen pals for about 15 years) He kindly pointed me in the direction of Karolyn.

She surprised me by showing up at my annual *It's a Wonderful Life* Christmas party. I was like a dazed schoolboy. She was so sweet and thoughtful. She signed all sorts of memorabilia for me and sat down and visited with me and answered a thousand questions I had about the film.

That night we just hit it off and a friendship blossomed. She invited my wife and I to visit her in Kansas and she graciously attended several other Christmas parties that I hosted in the years ahead. She has always been kind and generous to me and has even helped me out of a jam or two when she didn't have to.

In short, thanks to *It's a Wonderful Life*, I was blessed with the greatest gift of all—a very special friend. It's fitting—a film about the importance and value of friendship blessed me with the sweetest of friends. And it goes without saying that although we can't see each other as often, there is nothing I would not do for her. She is a beautiful woman and in my opinion, a national treasure. Thanks, Jimmy, for helping me find her. Thanks Clarence! You were right—no man is a failure who has a friend.

Sincerely,
Jerry Baker

Potter's Rich and Savory Breakfast Casserole

Spray a 9″ × 13″ pan with cooking spray.
Butter 6 slices of bread, then cube and line pan for crust.
Combine:
8 eggs (beaten)
4 cups milk
1 tsp dry mustard

Spread 4 cups shredded cheddar cheese over the bread. Sprinkle with diced ham, bacon, chopped onions—any topping you like. Pour eggs over all and cover with foil. Refrigerate overnight. Cover with foil and bake in a preheated 350-degree oven for 1 hour. Remove foil and bake for 10 more minutes.

A behind-the-scenes birthday party for Lionel Barrymore

JOSEPH'S VOICE

George fought the battle of Bedford Falls.

POTTER:

George Bailey is . . . the smartest one of the crowd, mind you,
a young man who has to sit by and watch his friends go places,
because he's trapped. Yes sir, trapped into frittering his life away
playing nursemaid to a lot of garlic eaters.

ZUZU'S *Sneak Peek*

*I*n the scene with George Bailey in Potter's office, you have to notice some little things that Capra put in. First, George is in a really low chair so he looks so much smaller than Mr. Potter. But then also look at the little skull on Potter's desk with the chain hanging from it. That was Capra's way of saying Potter wanted to get a chain around George Bailey. Also, take a close look at Potter's forehead. He is wearing a skullcap that makes his forehead look bigger and more intimidating. If you look closely, you can see the line of the skullcap.

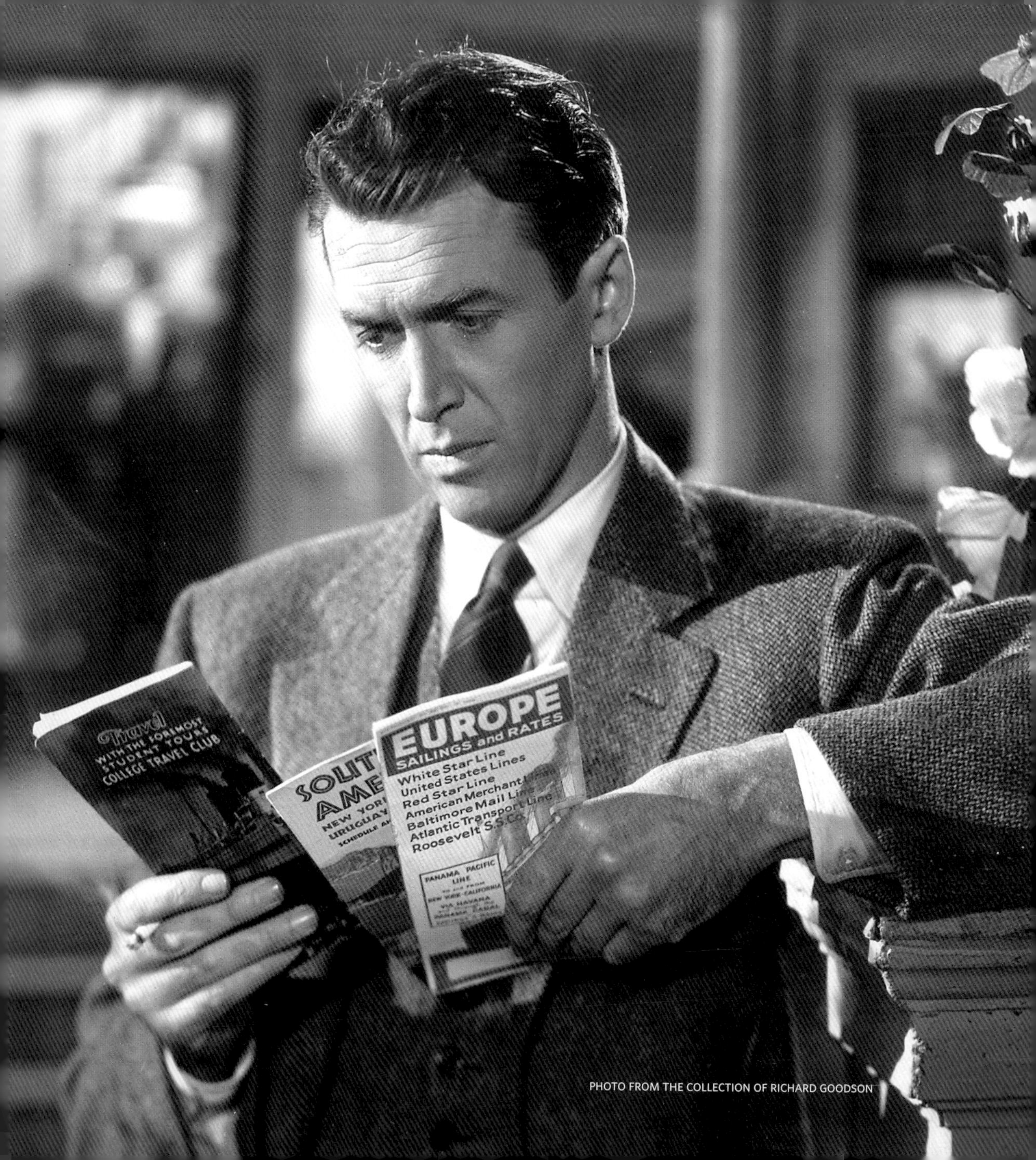

PHOTO FROM THE COLLECTION OF RICHARD GOODSON

SCENE
~~Three~~

JOSEPH'S VOICE:

Now you've probably already guessed that George
never leaves Bedford Falls.

I just wanted to see the

Karolyn as a young mother

L. to R. Back row: Haleen, Kylan, Karolyn, Deena, and Craig

L. to R. Front Row: Chris, John, and Carey

house where I grew up...

At one point after I was married to Hal and my first daughter was born, I told Hal I wanted to go back to Los Angeles and at least see my old life. So we packed up our car and drove all the way to California. I didn't want to see the studios. I really didn't care about that. I just wanted to see the house where I grew up, my dad's grocery store. . . . I guess I just needed to see it all before I could let it go.

When we got back to Missouri, I realized I had to put the past behind me and just focus on my life now. Soon I had two girls, and I started a dress shop in downtown El Dorado Springs.

After struggling with my husband's lack of responsibility for years, I realized that our marriage was really over. We divorced, and I moved to Kansas City and began the life of a single mother. That was a challenge—two little girls and a job at a doctor's office with long hours.

Not long after that, I met Mike on a blind date. He was a single dad with three kids. We married in July 1969, and we had two children of our own. So, we were like the Brady Bunch in a house with seven kids!

Zuzu

STAGE
14

The four Bailey kids get together for a reunion at Stage 14 where many scenes were shot for *IAWL*.

days long behind me.

Until all the renewed interest in the film, I really had not sat down and watched it. I put those Hollywood days long behind me. I had a lot of movie memorabilia in trunks in the basement. Once in a while one of the children would take a photo to "Show and Tell." So it was very interesting how the major push for me to get back on the road came from the Target Company. They created a whole ad campaign based on a reunion of the Bailey kids. They got us together and sent us on tour. Oh, that was fun! I hadn't seen them for so long! Now we have a wonderful bond that keeps us very close. And I had a part of my old life back. It was amazing after all those years.

And then there were three

Larry Simms (Petey Bailey) got his wings June 17, 2009. We had some fun times together, especially during the days of the tour we did for the Target stores. Larry lived most of his last years in Thailand. He loved the ocean and he said that all his life he always lived no farther than 20 miles from the sea.

ZUZU: Hi, Daddy.

GEORGE: Well, what happened to you?

ZUZU: I won a flower. . . .

GEORGE: Wait now.
Where do you think you're going?

ZUZU: Want to give my flower a drink.

GEORGE: All right, all right. Here, give Daddy the flower.
I'll give it a drink.

She shakes her head and presses the flower to her.
A few petals fall off. She picks them up.

ZUZU: Look, Daddy . . . paste it. . . .

GEORGE: Yeah, all right. Now I'll paste this together. . . .
There it is, good as new.

ZUZU'S *Sneak Peek*

I remember how big Jimmy Stewart's hand was—huge; it covered my whole face. And I was like, "Ahh!" If you look carefully at the shot, you can see that I peek and notice that he is putting the flower petals in his pocket. We shot that scene probably 20 times, and Capra could have taken that out. I think there is a reason he left it in there, because he was methodical about things like this. I think the reason he left it in there—he may have even told me to look at it; I'm not sure—I think that it's all about the fact that I knew my daddy wasn't perfect, but I loved him. It was a relationship.

There are relationships throughout the movie; all kinds of intricate relationships, and this was between a father and his daughter. He carries me everywhere. Tommy's the little one, but I'm sick, and he carries me everywhere and I'm always with him and he's always concerned about Zuzu, so there's a reason for that.

There are relationships throughout the movie; all kinds of intricate relationships …

85

Karolyn and Jimmy Stewart in New York getting ready to attend an awards ceremony for Jimmy and his leading ladies

Zuzu's Petals

Something that stands out as an icon for the movie is the theme I'd call "Zuzu's Petals." A simple flower in this film becomes the catalyst for parental concern and protectiveness; it allows us to see the trust that a child can have for a parent, even as she is developing her own view of the world; it is a springboard for the power of imagination; and it evokes the fear of loss as well as the joy of regaining something we feared was gone forever.

We learn of the petals in a scene where Zuzu, sick in bed because she had braved the cold to protect the flower she had won, asks her father to "paste" the dropped petals. As parents often do, George shields her. It is a sad reality that flowers can't be fixed and George chooses to turn away and put the petals in his pocket rather than let Zuzu know this. He hands back a flower that looks whole. Zuzu, perhaps not really deceived, thanks him as if she believes he has the magical power to fix anything that could ever go wrong. Zuzu doesn't want to sleep, but he knows she needs to rest and he tells her she can dream about the flower and it "will be a whole garden." In this scene, little Karolyn Grimes, as Zuzu, creates a timeless portrayal of a child with her own strong will but also with a devotion to the father she adores and who clearly adores her in return. The Bailey family is not perfect, but it does have love at its foundation.

Later, when George has asked for and been given the gift of seeing a world without him, he searches his pocket for the petals but they are not there. This is his first awareness that if he had not lived, his children would never have existed either. It is a profound moment in the film as we see the confusion and pain in Jimmy Stewart's face. He will have to endure much more before he begs to have his life back. The petals are a focus again in the joyous scene when George is eventually brought back to reality. He confirms that he's alive again, busted jaw and all, by finding the petals back where they belong, in his pocket.

Everyone has family issues and we all, at some point, probably wish we could escape from that reality. To me, Zuzu's petals are a reminder that even the reality of a flower that can't be fixed is better than an escape to non-existence. Zuzu's message is timeless.

Elizabeth Wellburn

TUE, 15 DEC 2009

I really want to let you know the joy my family and I get watching *It's a Wonderful Life* each Christmas. It is my favorite movie of all time (and my wife's also I believe). There are so many positives from the movie, I wouldn't know where to begin. But I always feel close to my family and loved ones after watching it.

Sometimes we'll say lines from the movie. . . . When we find something in our pocket we'll pull it out and say "Zuzu's petals!!!" Ha! A great line in the movie and one that reminds me of my love for my children as well. The movie is a huge reminder of all the blessings the Lord has given us.

God Bless,
Chris Clark

Good for one prayer

When my daughter Mandy was in first grade, she gave me a coupon that was "good for one prayer." I couldn't help thinking of it as my own special "Zuzu's petals," and I keep it in my wallet to this day. I hope it will be there if I ever really need that one special prayer.

John Mencl

PETE:
Daddy, how do you spell "Hallelujah"?

GEORGE (shouts):
How should I know? What do you think I am, a dictionary?

92

Aunt Tilly's Fresh Fruit Christmas Torte

1 package refrigerated sugar cookie dough
11 oz cream cheese, softened
⅓ cup sugar
3 Tbsp milk
2 Tbsp orange rind

Glaze
1 cup sugar
2 Tbsp cornstarch
Salt (dash)
¾ cup water
1 cup orange juice
¼ cup lemon juice
1 tsp orange rind
1 tsp lemon rind

....

Preheat oven to 350 degrees. Make the crust by rolling ½ package of cookie dough in a thin layer in each of two 12″ pizza pans. The dough must be cold and plenty of flour used while rolling it out. Prick dough with fork and bake according to package directions. Cool. To prepare filling: whip cream cheese, sugar, milk, and grated rind together. Spread evenly over top of crust. Decorate with fresh fruit in concentric circles and top with glaze.

Glaze
- Combine sugar, cornstarch and salt. Add water, orange juice, and lemon juice. Bring to a boil and cook 1 minute. Add rinds. Cool. Pour evenly over top of fruit.
- Chill and serve. Amount: 2 tortes equal serves 20.

PETE: Is Daddy in trouble?

JANIE: Shall I pray for him?

MARY: Yes, Janie, pray very hard.

TOMMY: Me too?

MARY: You too, Tommy.

This scene shows a troubled Mary and was used for publicity; however, it was cut from the final movie.

Christopher traveled quite a distance to meet Karolyn at an event after he learned she was going to use his poem in her book.

A Poem of Hope

Here I live in the city of abandoned dreams
Where no one thinks positive and only screams
A place where sin is consumed day and night
There is a spiritual battle that I must fight
A place where put-downs echo from my past
Why can't I let go, and forgive and move on fast?
I need to break the chain of what's holding me back
Show no lack of confidence and show no slack
Now, I see the rain and clouds clearing away
The sun peaks through the clouds trying to shine today
The sad sky of gray dissolves out of sight
Letting in the joyful sky of blue shine bright
The sound of celestial music plays in my ear
Giving me hope, the sound of no fear
And what once was an expression of sadness
Now cheerfully changes into the expression of gladness
A place where people once hurt and now hurt no more
The sound of their laughter and bliss galore
My heart and soul now finding warmth and peace
Bitterness, anger, and depression now decrease
And where once was this city of abandoned dreams
Is now a place where dreams fulfilled and sins redeemed.

Christopher Ian Hill

"Welcome home,

by Clay Eals

The most touching parts of any movie emerge when the words and images seem to transcend sound and sight and engage all our senses. For me, one of the best such scenes in "It's a Wonderful Life" comes almost exactly halfway through the film. It's after George aborts his big-city trip with Mary and, with her assent, invests their saved cash to keep alive the family business and salve the spirits and consciences of their hometown friends during a bank run.

A rain-soaked George walks that night to the abandoned Granville mansion, not knowing it has been hastily transformed into a honeymoon suite. With moments of startling visual composition, sweet humor, visceral weather and dreamy music (from Hawaii, no less), the scene shifts inside the house to an approach that is as straightforward as can be.

Hands raised to his hips and eyebrows lifted above his saucer eyes, George stammers a silent "What . . .?" while the camera tracks his deliberate gaze around the front room. Then, dead center in the frame, springs the stunning visage of Mary, just her head and shoulders, tears welling in her eyes, beaming with joy. While looking straight at George (and almost directly at us), she says with a lilt that is both earthly and heavenly, "Welcome home, Mr. Bailey."

Mr. Bailey."

100

For any man who has genuinely loved a woman, and vice versa, this scene is instantly evocative. But it doesn't stop there.

What follows is a kiss—a real one, not fake like so many of the era—along with the warmest embrace imaginable. Dumbstruck, George is palpably gentle, while Mary, her arms raised over his shoulders in a complete circle, her fingers stroking the hair at the base of his head, her lips mere inches from his ear, speaks gratefully of the profound fulfillment of a wish. She snuggles and nestles her cheek and chin into his neck, and a lifetime bond is sealed, impermeable, inviolate. They are, indeed, home.

Countless others glorify the film's so-called telephone scene 15 minutes earlier as a perfect expression of passion overcoming ambition, and no question, it is a powerful juncture in the story. But the incurable romantic in me is fueled far more by the later intimacy. It is truly the point at which two become one. I look forward to it every time.

Clay Eals
Seattle, Washington

Clay Eals addressing an audience

While my book on Karolyn, *Every Time a Bell Rings: The Wonderful Life of Karolyn Grimes,* was wholly journalistic, I am honored and grateful that she and I also became the closest of friends. She possesses an undeniable and contagious zest for life, and it is one of the greatest gifts of my life to have shared so much significant time with her. Thank you, Karolyn, and much love to you.

IOI

She's a Peach Dessert

1 29-oz can of sliced peaches, drained
5 slices white bread
1½ cups sugar
2 Tbsp flour
1 egg
1 stick butter, melted

....

Preheat oven to 350 degrees. Place fruit in baking dish (8″ × 8″). Cut crust from bread and cut each slice into fine strips. Place strips over peaches. Mix sugar, flour, egg, and butter. Blend well and pour over bread strips. Bake 35 to 45 minutes or until golden brown.

SCENE

Four

ERNIE: Don't look now, but there's something funny going on over there at the bank, George, I've never really seen one, but that's got all the earmarks of a run.

PASSERBY: Hey, Ernie, if you got any money in the bank, you better hurry.

MARY: George, let's not stop. Let's go! . . .

GEORGE: Just a minute, dear. Oh-oh . . .

In the early 1970s, the copyright was allowed to lapse on *It's a Wonderful Life* so the movie went into public domain. Television stations across America could show the film for free. Therefore the movie was played over and over during that period. That is how people were introduced to the story. That is also the time people realized how much they wanted to watch it and enjoy it every Christmas.

It was unbelievable!

In 1980, while I was living in Kansas, someone knocked on my door and asked me if I was that little girl, Zuzu, in the movie. He said he was a local reporter and wanted to do a story on the film and wondered if I would give him an interview. That was the beginning of what today is a second career for me. I said, "Sure." After that, there were more interviews and I stated getting fan mail. It was unbelievable! I was shocked. I started doing local appearances. While still raising kids, I pretty much stayed in the area doing talks about the film.

In 1989, my 18-year-old son took his own life. After that, each day seemed like a walk through a dream. I had to remain strong for the rest of the family. I prayed for that strength.

Karolyn at a groundbreaking for a grade school in Florida

I just started writing letters to my son and telling him how sorry I was that I did not realize how badly he was hurting. I would ask him to forgive me and tell him how much I loved him. I did this for about a year. I had to deal with the what if's . . . or the why didn't I's . . . So much guilt.

It was about three months before I could go out of the house, even the grocery store. I had a lot of friends who helped in that way. Then when I finally did go out, it seemed like I always was looking for him. That finally stopped with time. I had choices . . . I could either let it destroy me or I could finally face the actual physical pain. I would cry at the strangest times. But life like that was not healing for me. So my choice was to realize that I LOVED HIM SO MUCH and I reflected that I DID THE BEST I COULD at the time raising him. When I started feeling sorry for myself, that is when I would reach deep inside and those still . . . to this day . . . are my mantras.

He was in a lot of pain and I would never want that for him…so I realized that I had to let him go. He is in a place where he is happy. I

Karolyn at a speaking engagement in Detroit

miss him so much but I know in my heart that I am feeling pain because of myself not him . . . I am able to realize that he is on another adventure now and he is out of the terrible pain he was suffering from. At last he can be happy. . . .

Another thing I started doing was to do lots of volunteer work. . . . I was in a place where I felt bad about myself . . . but when I helped others, I got love back and I started feeling better about myself. Today I feel that the work I do one-on-one with people is still the mission that I am to be on. . . . I get much comfort from the smiles from dear people, like me, who have experienced the pain of losing a loved one.

I will never get over the pain, but it eases with time. I have learned to live with it. When my son's best friend got married, he and his wife dedicated the reception to my son.

Every Christmas, I donate to a fund at his school in his memory. That is my gift to him . . . to help another young man get an education. I don't ever want him forgotten. That is my way of telling him I will always love him.

Eventually, I was able to function again and to really appreciate the movie that showed how every one of us has value and that we have great power within us to help others. This served as a healing for me. Life is such a wonderful gift that we have been given.

In the early 1990s, my husband was diagnosed with cancer. After 25 years of marriage, I would lose him to this dreadful disease.

It was at this time, I decided to take advantage of the opportunity to travel and meet people and give back to them some of what the movie had meant to me. The love folks have for this film and for this little girl, Zuzu, has brought me healing.

Karolyn Grimes
"Zuzu"

GEORGE:

Now we can get through this thing all right. We've got to stick together, though. We've got to have faith in each other.

It's a Wonderful Life holds a very special place in my heart. This movie was introduced to our family by my husband Gary. We looked forward to watching it together many times during the Christmas season year after year. We enjoyed it, but didn't embrace the important message of supportive, loving family and friends until Gary became terminally ill. In his final weeks, *It's a Wonderful Life* played non-stop for him and all who visited simply to strengthen our faith in God and our love for all the many friends that lifted our family up during an extremely difficult time. If angels are sent to support and guide us, I believe that God provides His angels in the bodies of those He places in our lives when we are most weakened and in need.

Bev Fishleigh

III

MARTINI:

I own the house. Me, Giuseppe Martini.*
I own my own house.
No more we live like pigs in thisa
Potter's Field.

Karolyn with Mrs. Martini,
Argentina Brunetti

My son and daughter-in-law just bought their first home. I wanted to give them a basket of bread, salt, and a bottle of wine. I loved how the Bailey Building & Loan gave the basket to all of the people that they financed a home for. Do you know what they said when they welcomed the new homeowners to their first home? I think it was *"Bread, so that you never go hungry; salt, so that your life will always have flavor"* or something like that. I cannot remember what they said about the wine. I love the movie so much! Every time I watch it I see something new in it. Wasn't it so funny that it was not a big hit when they released it?

Donna Marie Loverette

"Bread, so that you

never go hungry ..."

GEORGE: Aw, now, Ed . . . what'll it take till the bank reopens? What do you need?

ED: Well, I suppose twenty dollars.

GEORGE: Twenty dollars. Now you're talking. Fine. Thanks, Ed. All right, now, Mrs. Thompson. How much do you want?

MRS. THOMPSON: But it's your own money, George.

GEORGE: Never mind about that. How much do you want?

MRS. THOMPSON: I can get along with twenty, all right.

ZUZU'S *Sneak Peek*

*S*eneca Falls is one of the places I go every year. This little town up in the Finger Lakes area of New York has become a really big part of my life. The first time I saw it, I couldn't believe how much it looks like Bedford Falls, especially the steel bridge across the canal! There is even a renovated historic Hotel Clarence. Every year in December, since 2001, I help the town host an *It's a Wonderful Life* festival. We give out a George Bailey humanitarian award, and we have a 5K run in the snow and just lots of fun. People dress up like people from the movie so you might meet George Bailey in the street or even bump into Mary. We have a parade, and I meet and greet people. We celebrate the film, and at the close of each festival, on Sunday at 4 PM, all the churches in town ring their bells to honor the memory of the loved ones we have lost. I'm so happy to help the community. I know they've had some hard times.

The Similarities between

Bedford Falls and Seneca Falls

The Similarities between Bedford Falls and Seneca Falls

http://www.therealbedfordfalls.com/therealbedfordfalls.php

- Seneca Falls and Bedford Falls are both mill towns.

- Seneca Falls had a grassy median same as the one George runs down in Bedford Falls with a movie theater located off to the side.

- Both communities boast Victorian Architecture and a large Italian population.

- The location is perfect: George's sister-in-law's father owns a glass factory in Buffalo, NY.

- Bailey's friend Sam wants to build a soybean processing plant outside of Rochester.

- The bank examiner wants to get back to Elmira on Christmas Eve.

- The train ran through Seneca Falls just as it did in Bedford Falls.

- The Bedford Falls High School was dedicated in 1927 the same year as the old Mynderse Academy was dedicated.

- In the film, the Bailey's Savings and Loan Association builds low cost housing called Bailey Park. In Seneca Falls, 19th Century factory owner

John Rumsey helped immigrant workers by lending them money and building low cost housing. It is still known as Rumseyville today.

- A local businessman named Norman J. Gould owned Gould Pumps, and was one of the richest men in town. He drove his car with license number NJG1. Norman Gould also had great control over politics and economics of the area. Much as Mr. Potter did in the movie. Norman could send someone to fight in the military or retain them for his factory.

*W*hen Karolyn first came to Seneca Falls, my daughter and husband and I waited in line with so many others to get her autograph. We took a photo of her with my daughter, quickly went and printed it, came back, and asked Karolyn to autograph it. I remember thinking how special she made us feel, and over the years I have seen over and over how she takes the time to show everyone they have value. She will always get up and take a photo with someone no matter how long the day has been. . . .

In early 2010, we had the idea to establish The Seneca Falls It's a Wonderful Life Museum in half of the IDEA Center, which is located in what was the first movie theater in Seneca Falls, built by Charles Fornesi in 1913. Karolyn was extremely supportive and provided us with just the right photographs and memorabilia. We started with one display case, now have five, and are always thinking about how to add more. Every time a new display case was donated to us, Karolyn chose more pieces from her collection to fill it.

In the museum, we see on a daily basis how Karolyn continues to touch the lives of so many people she will never meet. They feel special because Karolyn has chosen to share her collection and memories with them. Visitors are so happy to be surrounded by the memories and message of a timeless and timely film as they feel the presence of Zuzu, whose rose petals and life story have become a powerful symbol of hope.

Anwei S. Law

The Seneca Falls It's a Wonderful
Life Museum and *IDEA Center for
the Voices of Humanity*,
Seneca Falls, New York

PHOTOS BY ANWEI S. LAW

*M*y mother had kept many more items from this film than any other one that I was in. There were original photos, media clippings all preserved in a scrapbook. I eventually started collecting memorabilia from the film. At times I had a virtual museum in my home.

When the idea for the Seneca Falls It's a Wonderful Life Museum came along, I was thrilled. This wonderful little place in Seneca Falls, New York is where I have the opportunity to display some of my collectables. It is so important to me to have a permanent year-round place that people can share in the positive messages that Frank Capra wanted the world to know.

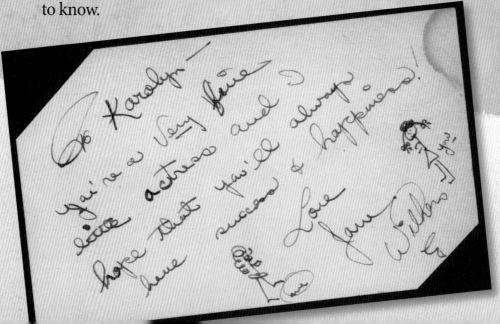

The Falls Salmon Spread

8 oz cream cheese
1 Tbsp capers
6 oz smoked salmon
4 green olives, chopped
1 tsp lemon juice
½ Tbsp Dijon mustard

....

Break up salmon and soften cream cheese with fork. Mix all together at least 24 hours before serving so that the flavors can blend. Serve with crackers of choice.

Hotel Clarence (top) —Inside the lobby of this hotel, the movie is projected year-round on the wall.

The Old Mill in Seneca Falls (below)

Main Street in Seneca Falls (right)

God put me here for a purpose . . .

I've written you before as I have found your life story to be a greater inspiration than *IAWL*, in many ways. I have made it a point to watch the movie at least once every year during the Christmas season. I have also tried to watch it with my kids since they were little. I've had my ups and downs in life, including surviving cancer, and whenever I felt down or thought "why me?" I have thought of *IAWL* and that God put me here for a purpose and that my life may have favorably affected and influenced others. That always lifted me up and made me realize that I had lots left to do with my life.

So, I hope this missive finds you well and in good spirits. . . . Your small part in the movie has had a big influence in my life.

God Bless,
Andy Redd

129

MAY 25, 2009

After a five year battle with Ovarian Cancer last Friday May 22nd at 3:50 AM, my mother went home to be with the Lord. . . . I share this with you because I know that she also enjoyed watching *It's a Wonderful Life* over the years and I know it made an impact on her life. . . . In looking at my mother's life of 72 years, had she not been here she would have left a big hole in the lives of many people. Karolyn, thanks so much for keeping the flame alive and sharing the Spirit of *It's a Wonderful Life*. More people need to know and understand just how precious they are and the importance they play in the lives around them.

David Kleier

keeping the flame alive

JUNE 2009

Dear David:

I am so sorry to hear about your mother. In a way she was like George Bailey. She faced adversity at times yet she kept on going because of the core values in her heart. . . . The grief of losing someone you love is real physical pain for a time but that will eventually lesson as life goes on. This Christmas will be a time when you can celebrate her memory as you and your family watch this beloved film and know that she will always be a part of that tradition.

Karolyn Grimes
"Zu Zu"

Indeed it is a wonderful life!

MONDAY, DECEMBER 22, 2008

I first saw the movie during the Christmas Holiday season of 1981, which had been a rather difficult year for me . . . my best friend had committed suicide. My wife and I learned that our jobs in Boston were being eliminated, and we had made the decision to move to Atlanta in an effort to "start over. . . ." Not really having anything else to do, and not really feeling the "Christmas Spirit" that night, we settled in for our first exposure to the film. Needless to say, we were both in tears at the end, and have now watched the movie every year since. . . . Indeed, it IS a wonderful life!"

David S. Young, Ed.S.
Decatur, GA

GEORGE:

God . . . God . . . Dear Father in Heaven, I'm not a praying man, but if you're up there and you can hear me, show me the way. I'm at the end of my rope. Show me the way, God.

133

ZUZU'S *Sneak Peek*

*T*his scene in *It's a Wonderful Life*—in Martini's bar, in which George Bailey says he's at the end of his rope and he prays to God to "show me the way"— was Jimmy's favorite scene of the film. . . . He was very emotional in this scene, and the first take was great, but director Frank Capra wanted to capture the moment better. Capra shot it several more times, with lesser results. Finally, in the editing room, Capra got what he wanted. This was in the days before zoom lenses. Frame by frame, Capra intricately cropped and enlarged the image to create the effect of zooming in on Jimmy's face. A devout Presbyterian, Jimmy felt this moment in the shooting especially affected him. He felt his emotions were over the top and that it was almost real. And I would agree. It is one of the best scenes in the film.

134

PHOTOS FROM THE COLLECTION OF RICHARD GOODSON

"Show me the way, God"

DECEMBER 30, 2011

I don't know if this email still works, but I just watched *It's a Wonderful Life*, which I haven't seen in maybe ten years, and while flooded with these emotions and crying a bit, I thought I'd look up "Zuzu" on IMBD and see what other movies she's been in, and they had this email listed.

Well, I'm not even sure what I want to say other than I find myself in a similar position to George Bailey this holiday season with a crippling financial burden and despair nipping at my heels and I often echo George's prayer "please God, show me the way." . . . I just wanted to acknowledge the power of the film, and of storytelling, for people to share hope and love, even between strangers and across so many years.

So, even though I only "know" the six-year-old you, I just wanted to thank you.

Maybe someday I will hear a bell ring—and it might be me earning my wings, God willing.

Hugs,
William Meyer

I was a funeral director who spent more time at work than most. A great deal of tragic deaths had come all at once, many babies. . . . One day, during visitations a stranger called me to the lounge with the TV on. She said "Sit with me for a while." I did and we watched *It's a Wonderful Life*. The scene in the bar when George said, "I'm at the end of my rope," struck a nerve. Tears fell like never before and she said, "You're going to be fine," squeezed my hand and left. I watched the rest of the movie and sobbed like a baby.

The next day it seemed everyone was telling me I meant a great deal to them. Families I served in the past bumped into me and gave me an extra hello, or it just seemed that way. It was then that I realized I was making a difference in a small way. To this day I share "Baileyism" to everyone making sure they understand that even just one thing they do can change lives. I watch that movie 2-3 times every Christmas, and without a doubt it is My Favorite Movie!

David Rousculp

137

Two of Karolyn's grandchildren—
Bailey (left) and Avery

The Sweetness of Life
Chocolate Oatmeal Cake

1 cup quick-cooking oatmeal
1 stick butter
1⅓ cup boiling water
1½ cup sugar
2 eggs
1 tsp vanilla
1 cup flour
½ cup Hershey's Cocoa
1 tsp baking soda

....

Put oatmeal and butter in a mixing bowl, pour the boiling water over all.
Cover and let stand for 20 minutes. Add sugar, eggs, and vanilla. Beat well.
Add dry ingredients and mix well. Bake at 350 degrees for 35 minutes.

Frosting
½ cup butter
1 cup brown sugar
¼ cup milk
1¾ cup powdered sugar

....

Melt brown sugar and butter and boil for 2 minutes. Add milk and bring to a
boil. Cool. Add powdered sugar and spread.

SCENE
five

GEORGE:

Clarence! Clarence! Help me, Clarence. Get me back. Get me back. I don't care what happens to me. Only get me back to my wife and kids. Help me, Clarence, please! Please! I want to live again! . . . I want to live again. I want to live again. Please, God, let me live again.

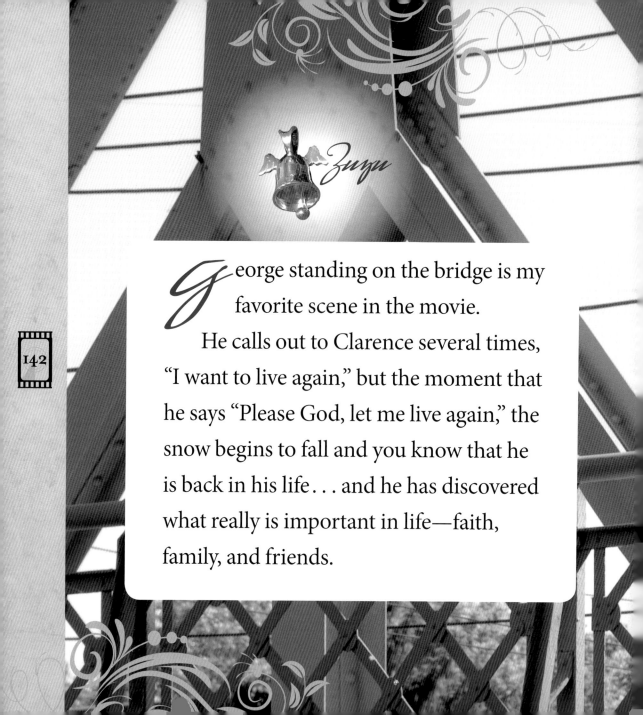

Zuzu

*G*eorge standing on the bridge is my favorite scene in the movie.

He calls out to Clarence several times, "I want to live again," but the moment that he says "Please God, let me live again," the snow begins to fall and you know that he is back in his life . . . and he has discovered what really is important in life—faith, family, and friends.

"Please God, let me live again."

143

The film is about a man who is about to commit suicide. Perhaps that is one of the reasons why it was not a success when it was released.

The film shows us that life can be dark, but if we practice helping each other, we begin to feel better about who we are. I learned that we have to take care of ourselves in order to take care of others. George Bailey cared about people and tried to make their lives better. The things in life that are the most important are not material things, but intangible things. Our faith and belief in God and our friends are very powerful tools to travel through this life. My feeling is that we each have an angel watching over us. We have been given the precious gift of the ability to make choices. So often, we are faced with challenges and it becomes difficult to make decisions.

George was not a praying man, but he asked for help—not for the $8,000. He just said, "I'm at the end of my rope. Show me the way, God." We often need help with our decisions. We have to learn to love ourselves. Mary and the children put a star on the top of the Christmas tree. Stars, angels, bells ringing, and the warmth of the love that we have for each other is a path to a wonderful life.

144

Karolyn,

I am 54 years old and have seen *It's a Wonderful Life* at least 54 times. I'm sure there are quite a few years where I have seen it more than once.

I had what for me was a profound experience when I watched it last holiday season. This is something that I assume you and most people got a long time age.

But when George is on the bridge and begs God for his life back, it occurred to me that in many ways his life was no different at that moment than it was that morning. But his character went from a place of fear, resentment and anger, to a place of acceptance and gratitude.

Sometimes I catch myself thinking, why do I feel good today? Today is not different than yesterday but I feel better. To me the answer is acceptance and gratitude.

God Bless ya,
Glynne Pisapia

PHOTO FROM THE COLLECTION OF RICHARD GOODSON

GEORGE:

My mouth's bleeding, Bert! My mouth's bleed . . .
(feeling in watch pocket) Zuzu's petals! Zuzu's . . .
they're . . . they're here, Bert! What do you know
about that?

Merry Christmas!

PHOTO FROM THE COLLECTION OF RICHARD GOODSON

Mouth-Watering Spinach Casserole

3 10 oz packages frozen chopped spinach, drained
1 (12 oz.) carton of sour cream
1 package dry onion soup mix

....

Heat oven to 350 degrees. Combine ingredients and mix well. Place in greased 1½ quart casserole and bake 30 minutes. Can be mixed the day before. Serves 8.

GEORGE:

Merry Christmas, emporium! . . .
Merry Christmas, you wonderful old
Building and Loan! . . .
Merry Christmas, Mr. Potter!

152

$\mathcal{M}$ovies at this time used cornflakes as snow. Capra realized he would have to dub the voices over the crunching of snow so he and his crew mixed up a concoction of foamite and Ivory Soap flakes and used a Ritter machine to blow it around. I loved that snow. I had grown up in California all my life so I had never seen snow—real or fake!

Ritter machines blowing artifical snow on the movie set.

PHOTO FROM THE COLLECTION OF RICHARD GOODSON

Snowy Strawberry Bread

1½ cups flour
1 cup sugar
1½ tsp cinnamon
½ tsp salt
½ tsp baking soda
2 eggs, beaten
½ cup oil
1 cup strawberries fresh mashed or frozen,
thawed and drained

....

Heat oven to 350 degrees. Mix together flour, sugar, cinnamon, salt, and soda. Combine eggs, oil, and strawberries. Add to dry ingredients. Pour into a greased and floured 9″ × 5″ loaf pan. Bake 50 to 60 minutes. Serve with strawberry butter.

Strawberry Butter
1 10-oz package frozen strawberries
1 cup soft butter
1 cup sifted powdered sugar

....

Combine ingredients and blend in mixer. Serve with strawberry bread. Makes 2½ cups.

POTTER:

Happy New Year to you—in jail! Go
on home—they're waiting for you!

Potter's Crabby Macaroni Casserole

½ cup butter

¼ cup chopped onions

½ cup flour

1 quart half and half, heated to boiling point

Salt (to taste)

Pepper (to taste)

2 Tbsp fresh lemon juice

4 cups canned crabmeat or use fresh crabmeat

3 9-oz packages frozen artichoke hearts cooked

2½ cups shell macaroni, cooked and drained

1 cup grated Gruyere cheese

1 cup grated Swiss cheese

155

....

Melt butter in a large saucepan. Add onion and sauté until golden,
Stir in flour, making a roux. Remove from heat and add half and
half, stirring vigorously until it thickens. Add extra flour if necessary.
Season with salt and pepper. Pour lemon juice over crabmeat. Toss
lightly. Combine crabmeat, artichoke hearts, macaroni, cheeses, and
cream sauce. Place in a 6-quart casserole. Bake at 350 degrees for 25 to
30 minutes. May be prepared 1 day ahead and refrigerated.
Serves 10—12.

I felt like a frog coming down the stairs on Jimmy's back! I had my arms wrapped around his throat and was literally hanging from his neck. He had Tommy under one arm and was holding Mary's hand with his other hand. My legs were wrapped around him like a frog. We did that take so many times, and I remember hanging on for dear life and just hoping I wouldn't fall off.

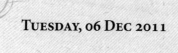

TUESDAY, 06 DEC 2011

My name is Sarah. I'm Deaf. One day my store manager told me that someone dropped something off for me, It was the picture of the *It's Wonderful Life* photo with your signature . . . I wept when I received the photo. I LOVED the movie and it's my number one favorite Christmas movie. Karolyn, you had made a huge impact on my life . . . I want you to know that I am forever grateful that there is somebody out there . . . who has a serving heart to other people like you.

Sarah

Zuzu

Phil Erklen, a dear friend, lives in Colorado Springs and is a man who helps people. . . mostly through music. He has a music studio that is state of the art, and he has brought me into the Springs to speak a number of times. That is how I met him. Phil has been a fan of the movie forever, and he practices giving of himself and touching lives in a very positive way. His entire life is pretty much made up of helping others.

For the last 10 years, if he sees a doctor or a flight attendant or a waitress or anyone that he has interactions with, he asks them if they like the film. In the end most do, and he loves to surprise them by sending them one of my photos. He orders from me and then send these items to the people he has encountered in life. That is how Sarah in the previous email got the photo. It was Phil who dropped the photo off. He is like a little Santa Claus, and he touches so many lives through his studio and his kindness.

■ I arranged a tribute concert for Karolyn in 2000. She was under the impression that she was coming to Colorado Springs to conduct one of her presentations (which she did). At the end of her presentation, I surprised her with the playing of a piece composed in her honor.

Phil Erklen

HARRY:

Good idea, Ernie.
A toast . . . to my big brother, George.
The richest man in town!

HOPE

v. to cherish a desire with anticipation.

Merriam Webster's Collegiate Dictionary

Zuzu

$\mathcal{I}$n 1997, I met Chris Brunell. I was speaking at a convention, and he had never seen the film. I was shocked. He is a clinical psychologist, and when he finally saw the film, he realized what my "mission" really is. Our meeting was no accident, and we fell in love. We decided to travel this path of life together. We have had many adventures all over the world. His background and input have helped me to help others.

ZUZU:

Look, Daddy. Teacher says, every time
a bell rings an angel gets
his wings.

"Every time a bell rings an angel gets his wings."

When Karolyn says, "Every time a bell rings an angel gets his wings" from the Christmas tree scene at the very end of the movie, this is significant because . . . Clarence got his wings and succeeded in his mission to make George realize how important life is and how his own life affects the lives of those around him. This applies to all of us.

Phil Erklen

165

"Every time a bell rings an angel gets his wings" is a comforting saying. We all have lost someone dear or very special to us. It's nice to hope that whenever we hear bells ringing that they are ringing for our loved ones and friends, letting us know that they have earned their wings and are somewhere up above in the most beautiful place one could ever imagine. A place where there is an over-abundance of love, peace, beauty, and serenity. . . .

I also like the scene when Clarence shows George Bailey what life would be like if he had never been born. Everyone's lives are in some way intertwined. If our parents had never been born, we wouldn't be here. Karolyn wouldn't have been here to make her movies, which give us all many hours of enjoyment. I wouldn't have met her and have such a wonderful friend. . . .

I connected with Karolyn actually through doll collecting. I've always watched *It's a Wonderful Life* every holiday season. I have the DVD and video so I can watch it anytime of the year. One day when I was reading a doll magazine, I saw an ad for the Zuzu doll. Of course I had to have it for my collection! In the ad it mentioned about Karolyn's husband dying of cancer. I wrote Karolyn a little note, expressing my sympathy. I ordered the doll. I had made Karolyn a beaded gingerbread house and filled it with homemade peanut brittle.

I never dreamed that I would receive a personal response from Karolyn. To my surprise, I received a lovely thank you note plus five autographed photos. I was just thrilled and I will always treasure those gifts.

A few months had gone by, when I received another little letter from Karolyn asking me how I was doing. Suffice it to say the rest is history. We've been corresponding ever since.

Continued on page 170

167

Potica

Dough
Mix together (with no water)
1 box Pillsbury Hot Roll mix plus dry yeast
2 Tbsp sugar
Mix the following and add to the dough mix:
2 Tbsp oil
1 egg
1 cup hot water

....

Knead a good 5 minutes so it is not sticky. Lightly flour both sides, cover, and let rise for 45 minutes.

Filling
Mix well:
4 cups finely ground walnuts
1 egg
8 oz honey
5 heaping Tbsp of sugar
¾ cup evaporated milk (or ½ a large can)
1 egg
1 cup hot water

On a floured cloth, stretch dough into a rectangular shape. (It will be stretched thin.) Spread filling to the ends. Pick up the ends of the cloth and roll it up. Break or cut into loaf-size pieces (usually 3 pieces). Pinch cut ends so filling doesn't come out. Put into well-greased loaf or bread pan. Let rise for another ⅓ hour.

Bake at 325 degrees for 50 minutes. When removed from the oven and still warm, brush the tops with butter.

Little did I know that in the year 2004, Karolyn's and my path would meet. In September, I had lost my mother and I received a lovely note from Karolyn. Then later on Karolyn had contacted me and said that she would be appearing at the Community Theatre in La Crosse, Wisconsin. She asked me if I could come down there and we could finally meet each other. It was just what I needed. . . .

Well, within a ring of a bell my husband and I were on our way to La Crosse, Wisconsin. I finally met Karolyn. We had corresponded for at least 11 years. It was like we knew each other our whole lives. . . . I felt that Karolyn and I were like two sisters who hadn't seen each other for a long time. We had a lot of catching up to do. We're both only children. I think of Karolyn as the sister who I never had. Needless to say we talked and talked with no loss of words. My husband Bill asked me if I was going to come up for air. Bill and I went to the theatre both nights.

Karolyn, being the special person that she is, had the cameraman put the camera on me. Boy, was I surprised when she introduced me to everyone there. . . .

During the holidays, I make Poticas and send them to Karolyn. . . .

Karolyn is to me and always will be a wonderful friend and the sister who I never had.

She's my Special Angel,
Frances (Francie) Skarich

3-14-2018
may you always
have a wonderful
life !

Frances (Francie) Skarich

Dear Karolyn—

I stumbled across your site accidentally today after my wife and I made a joyous decision this weekend. Therein is the story.

In January, our beloved Welsh corgi, Willa, died suddenly while romping in a beautiful, unseasonably warm field. She was thirteen and the embodiment of everything wonderful that a dog has to offer. She was smart and hardworking with a heart bigger than she was. She raised our daughter, fretted over all of us, and kept our younger corgi, Truman, in line. Her death left a huge hole in our lives.

When the pain subsided and it became obvious that Truman was lonely and continuing to grieve, we picked out another corgi pup from the breeder who has sold me dogs for 20+ years.

All was well until my wife and I—now empty nesters—could not agree on a name. We traded a lot of bad ideas as we worked through the alphabet. By the time we reached the Z names, I was on the verge of despair and then it hit me. The perfect name for this innocent little companion was my favorite name from my favorite movie: Zuzu.

The name is perfect in every corgi way. It's innocent, charming, unusual, and old-shoe-comfortable with wonderful associations. Each time we call her, we hear a bell ring and are certain that Willa earned her wings. We will also think of you and your wonderful character.

I attach a photo of Zuzu at six weeks. . . .

Very best wishes to you—
Stan Murphy
Portsmouth, Virginia

Hello,

I recently read an article about your life in a copy of *Power for Living* that I picked up at my church. I was introduced to the wonderful movie, *It's a Wonderful Life,* a number of years ago by a friend at work. Since that time, several of us have become huge fans, often quoting our favorite lines from the movie throughout the year. I'm sure it seems very strange to others to see middle-age guys quoting lines from a holiday movie in July!!

> *Since that time, the trials have not ceased, but my faith and continued hope in God have increased.*

Your life story sounds very tragic and at the same time touching. But the thing that impressed me the most was your faith and hope in God that sustained you through many storms and trials.

I cling very tightly to that same faith in God. Both of my parents died tragically of cancer, a few years ago. My father passed away on my parents' 43rd wedding anniversary and my mom died five years and one day later. Both of my parents were very strong Christians and it was the same faith that you have had that sustained not only my parents through their tragedy but my family as well.

Since that time, the trials have not ceased, but my faith and continued hope in God have increased. I just wanted to write and share with you, as others have, encouragement to cling to your faith . . . to *the old rugged cross.*" In the midst of pain and suffering, remember the words the great 18th century preacher and theologian, Jonathan Edwards said to his daughter before his death, " . . . it seems that it is the will of God that I am to leave you soon. Let this be an inducement for you to seek a father who will never fail you."

Thank you so much for the encouragement that your public profession of faith has given to others. May God continue to bless you!

Hope in God,

John Kessinger
Polo, Illinois

ZUZU'S *Sneak Peek*

I'm embarrassed about this scene at the end of the movie when we were singing "Auld Lang Syne" because I didn't know the words. I'm not sure Jimmy Stewart knew the words either! I think Capra left this in for a reason. Maybe to make it all look more real.

I never saw all these people in this big scene. Capra shot it in lots of different shots and then added them together. I do remember playing with that watch, though.

PHOTO FROM THE COLLECTION OF RICHARD GOODSON

Hark! The Herald Angels Sing

Hark! The herald angels sing,
"Glory to the newborn King;
Peace on earth, and mercy mild
God and sinners reconciled!"

LYRICS BY CHARLES WESLEY

Auld Lang Syne

Should auld acquaintance be forgot,
And never brought to mind?
Should auld acquaintance be forgot,
And days o' lang syne!

BASED ON A POEM BY ROBERT BURNS (1788)

I remember clearly praying for guidance through those troubled times. . . .

FRI JUNE 8, 2012

I remember clearly praying for guidance through those troubled times. . . . When someone from the "outside" validates what is on the "inside" of you as a person, you see your life as having meaning and potential beyond the day to day chores, trials, and seemingly unending frustrations and despair.

Terry Deinlein

$\mathcal{N}$o man is a failure who has friends." In a world which seems to only value the profit-driven successes of Mr. Potter and Sam Wainwright, George Bailey is a failure financially and appears to have also missed the boat of adventure and an engineering career that he had dreamt about his whole life. Instead, he has been fighting the daily battle of Bedford Falls. His small successes would help more people than he could imagine. By trying to do the right thing, rather than the get-rich quick thing, George holds up the principles of his father, and helps to keep people out of "Potter slums."

The movie contains so many timeless messages but the quote, *"No man is a failure who has friends"* is one of my favorites." As people face possible financial difficulties either in a difficult economy or due to the mistake of a bumbling relative, this quote reminds us of what is really valuable in the end, and gives us encouragement to carry on.

John Mencl

CLARENCE:

Strange, isn't it? Each man's life touches so many
other lives, and when he isn't around he leaves
an awful hole, doesn't he?

My legacy to the children

1998

Ms. Grimes, I have always loved the movie *It's a Wonderful Life*. I am now 32 and a father of two. I have a boy, 7, and a girl, 3.

I feel the message that the movie sends is more important now than ever before. These children are going to face adversities and challenges in a world that you and I won't even recognize in 20 years.

Part of my legacy to my children will be the memorabilia I will collect for them in the years to come. It is perhaps a feeble attempt to keep a message and spirit alive, yet I feel it is important that they carry the message of this story, the goodwill of the holiday season, and the promise of warm and compassionate tomorrows in their hearts.

Thank you for your efforts and investment in the future!

Richard Goodson

Richard is one of the leading collector's of *It's a Wonderful Life* memorabilia in the U.S.

2012

I purchased several items from Karolyn in the late 1990s. She responded with a personal note. Her warmth and willingness to connect with her fans really touched me. And now, almost 15 year later, I still look forward, with great anticipation, to our phone conversations and yearly visit.

With the rapid evolution of technology and the ever-increasing ways we have to communicate without truly connecting, the value of the individual contributions one man, one heart, one pure and enduring soul can make are often lost. This simple yet poignant quote, "Each man's life touches so many other lives . . ." speaks to the inherent connection we all share and the responsibility we have to each other.

183

In the scene where this quote is spoken, George is assured that one man's contributions, however small, good or bad, set a sequence in motion that has far-reaching consequences. It reminds each of us that the seemingly mundane interactions and tasks that we perform on a daily basis may truly end up meaning the world to someone we touch. Our life is a gift, an awesome responsibility, one that should be accepted with gratitude and humility. May we all find a way to contribute as meaningfully as George did.

Richard Goodson

Richard Goodson, with the youngest of his now three children, Matt.

*T*his film is just full of surprises… I realized a couple of years ago that the *Tom Sawyer* book only exists in heaven. This close up pic I took with my iPhone shows that the *Tom Sawyer* book in the film by Mark Twain was printed by Gutenberg. I believe Gutenberg was already in heaven a pretty long while after inventing the first printing press long before Mark Twain wrote *Tom Sawyer*.

John Mencl

Fade Out

CLARENCE:

No man is a failure who has friends.

Zuzu

This is a book from Karolyn as well as from Zuzu. I feel thankful and perhaps a little unusual in that I have, in essence, two personas. Being given the opportunity to go through a door to the past, present, and future, I am blessed. It is such a reward to be able to make people smile and feel good. When folks are in pain, I think it is a comfort to know that someone else has walked in their shoes and survived. I am and continue to be a survivor.

This wonderful film celebrates life by going into the depths of despair and rising to attain the greatest gift. That would be the gift of life. It gives us an opportunity to reflect on what really is important in our own lives. Sometimes the little painful things in life overshadow the big picture. George Bailey teaches us that we are important and that each of us has value. We all make a difference!

"... each of us has value."

Karolyn with
Carol Coombs Mueller
(Janie) in front of the
Seneca Falls Museum

Afterword

Karolyn and I met each other on the studio lot. When we weren't before the camera, we were sent to the studio school, which was right on the same stage. We then had time to talk and play and get to know each other a little. It was fun pretending I had a little sister. However it was a movie, and not real life. We didn't see each other again until 1993, when Target had their Christmas theme of "Building a Wonderful Life." The company got the four children together for a tour to promote some of their products. Since that time we've traveled to many states, sharing experiences with *IAWL*. Karolyn and I are good friends, keep in close contact, and have even visited in each other's home (different states!). Karolyn is a very wonderful, sweet, talented lady and I love to pretend she is my "sis."

Carol Coombs Mueller (Janie)

About the Author

KAROLYN GRIMES appeared in over 16 movies during the Golden Age of Hollywood. Her film credits include:

That Night with You, Universal, 1945

Pardon My Past, Columbia, 1946

Blue Skies, Paramount, 1946

Sister Kenny, RKO Radio Pictures, 1946

It's a Wonderful Life, Liberty Films/RKO Radio Pictures, 1946

The Private Affairs of Bel Ami, United Artists, 1947

Sweet and Low, Paramount, 1947

Philo Vance's Gamble, Producers Releasing Corporation, 1947

Mother Wore Tights, 20th Century Fox, 1947

Unconquered, Paramount, 1947

The Bishop's Wife, Samuel Goldwyn Productions/RKO Pictures, 1947

Albuquerque, Paramount-Clarion, 1948

Lust for Gold, Columbia, 1949

Rio Grande, Republic Studios, 1950

Honeychile, Republic Pictures, 1951

Hans Christian Anderson, RKO Radio Pictures, 1952